Prehistoric A

GIANT MEAT-EATING DINOSAURS

J 567.912 Wes
West, David
Giant meat-eating dinosaurs

$8.25
ocn922912479

WINDMILL BOOKS

New York

Published in 2016 by **Windmill Books**,
an Imprint of Rosen Publishing
29 East 21st Street, New York, NY 10010

Copyright © 2015 David West Children's Books

All rights reserved. No part of this book may be reproduced in any form without permission in writing from the publisher, except by a reviewer.

Designed and illustrated *by* David West

Cataloging-in-Publication Data
West, David.
Giant meat-eating dinosaurs / by David West.
p. cm. — (Prehistoric animals)
Includes index.
ISBN 978-1-5081-9026-4 (pbk.)
ISBN 978-1-5081-9027-1 (6-pack)
ISBN 978-1-5081-9028-8 (library binding)
1. Dinosaurs — Juvenile literature. 2. Predatory animals — Juvenile literature. 3. Carnivorous animals, Fossil — Juvenile literature. I. West, David, 1956-. II. Title.
QE861.5 W47 2016
567.912—d23

Manufactured in the United States of America

CPSIA Compliance Information: Batch #BW16PK: For Further Information contact Rosen Publishing, New York, New York at 1-800-237-9932

Contents

Acrocanthosaurus 4
Allosaurus 6
Carnotaurus 8
Cryolophosaurus 10
Giganotosaurus 12
Majungasaurus 14
Spinosaurus 16
Suchomimus 18
Tarbosaurus 20
Tyrannosaurus rex 22
Glossary and Timeline 24

● *Acrocanthosaurus* means "High-spined Lizard" after the tall spine bones along its back.

● *Acrocanthosaurus* was a powerful hunter. It had strong arms to hold on to its prey while it slashed with its razor-sharp teeth.

Acrocanthosaurus
ak-ro-KANTH-uh-SAWR-us

This large, sharp-toothed **predator** hunted giant, long-necked plant eaters that lived in the pine forests of the North American continent.

Acrocanthosaurus was about 39 feet (12 m) in length and weighed 6.6 tons (6 metric tons).

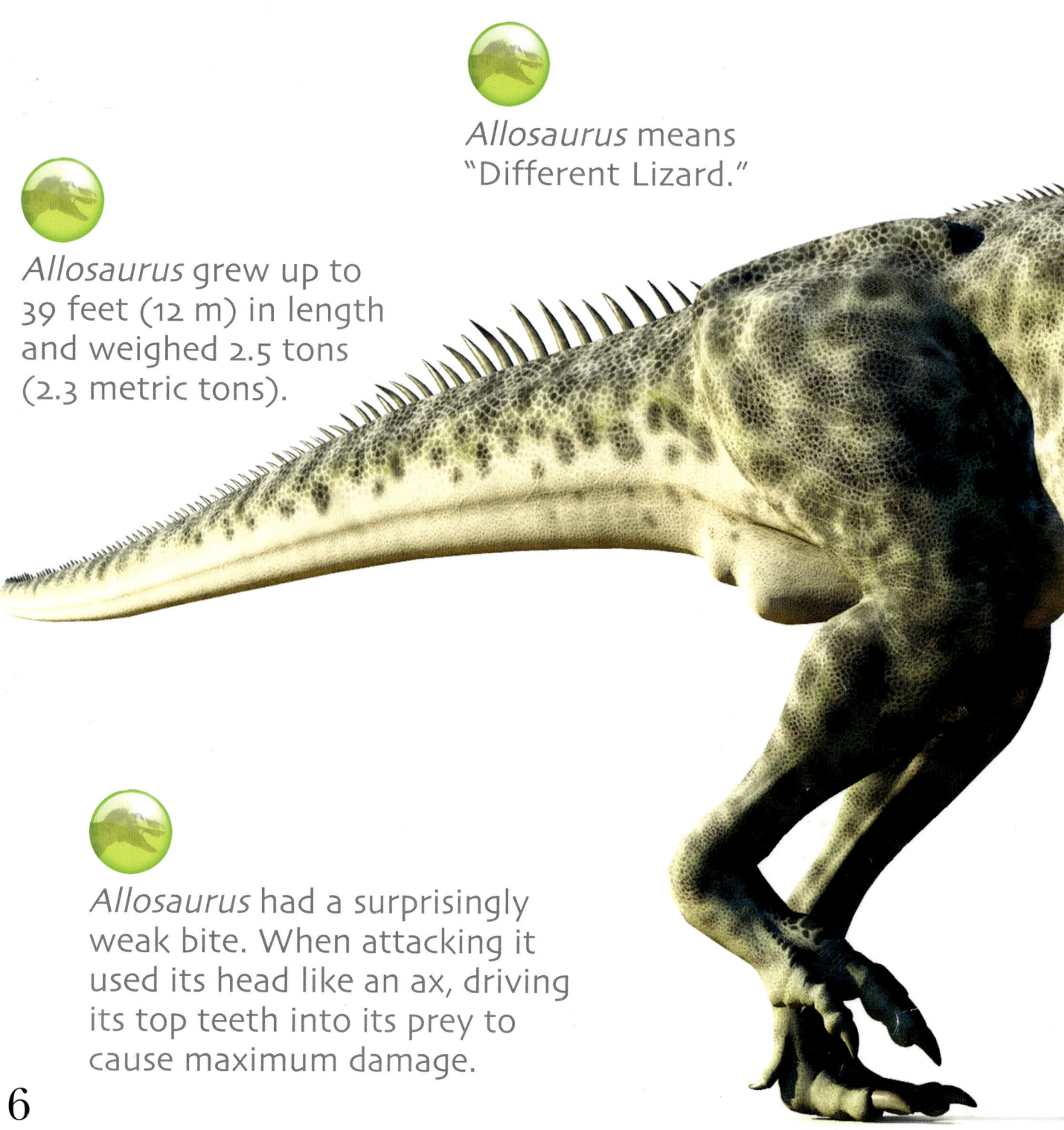

Allosaurus means "Different Lizard."

Allosaurus grew up to 39 feet (12 m) in length and weighed 2.5 tons (2.3 metric tons).

Allosaurus had a surprisingly weak bite. When attacking it used its head like an ax, driving its top teeth into its prey to cause maximum damage.

Allosaurus
AL-uh-SAWR-us

This speedy killer was the most common predator in North America 140 million years ago. It hunted on the plains, using surprise to ambush its prey.

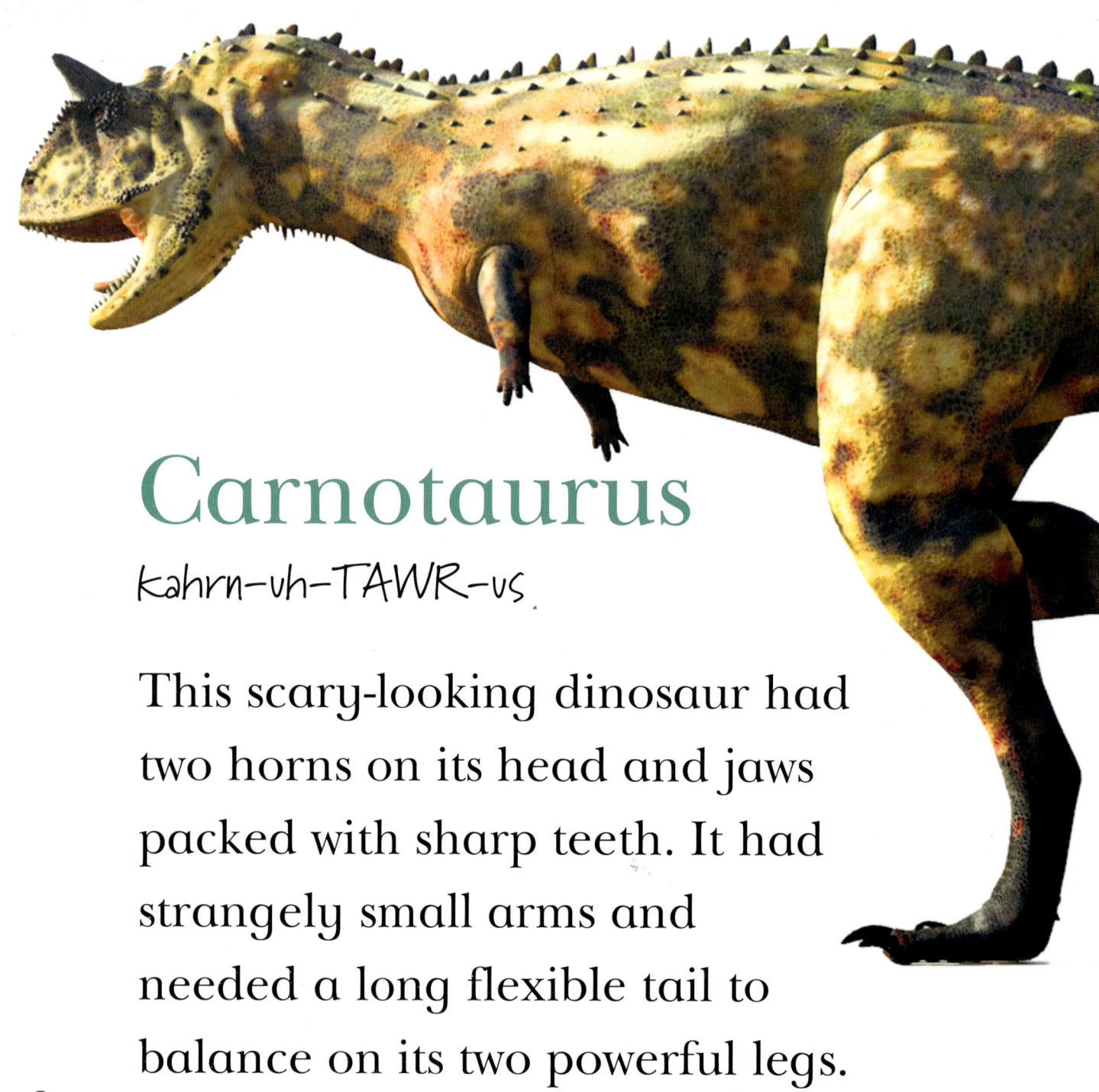

Carnotaurus

kahrn-uh-TAWR-us

This scary-looking dinosaur had two horns on its head and jaws packed with sharp teeth. It had strangely small arms and needed a long flexible tail to balance on its two powerful legs.

The eyes of *Carnotaurus* faced forward, which is unusual in a dinosaur. This meant it had eyesight similar to ours, which would have made it a good hunter.

Carnotaurus means "Meat-eating Bull" after the horns on its head.

Carnotaurus lived in South America and was 26 feet (8 m) long and weighed about 2.9 tons (2.6 metric tons).

Cryolophosaurus
cry-o-LOF-o-SAWR-us

This giant predator hunted plant eaters such as *Glacialisaurus* in southern lands now called Antarctica.

Cryolophosaurus used to be known as *Elvisaurus* because its crest looked like Elvis Presley's **cowlick**. The crest was probably used for display to impress females.

Cryolophosaurus means "Cold-crest Lizard" after the crest on its head and its discovery in cold Antarctica.

Cryolophosaurus was about 26 feet (8 m) in length and weighed around 1 ton (907 kg).

Giganotosaurus was about 43 feet (13 m) in length and weighed 6 tons (5.4 metric tons).

Giganotosaurus
ji-ga-note-uh-SAWR-us

Giganotosaurus was one of the biggest of the giant meat eaters. This massive predator hunted the plains of South America for large, long-necked **titanosaurs**.

For such a large beast, *Giganotosaurus* had a surprisingly small brain, the size and shape of a banana.

Giganotosaurus means "Giant Southern Lizard."

 *Majungasaurus* was named after the place where it was found, which was Mahajanga, in Madagascar.

 Fossil evidence has shown that these ferocious dinosaurs fought to the death and ate each other.

Majungasaurus was about 19.5 feet (6 m) in length and weighed 1.2 tons (1.1 metric tons).

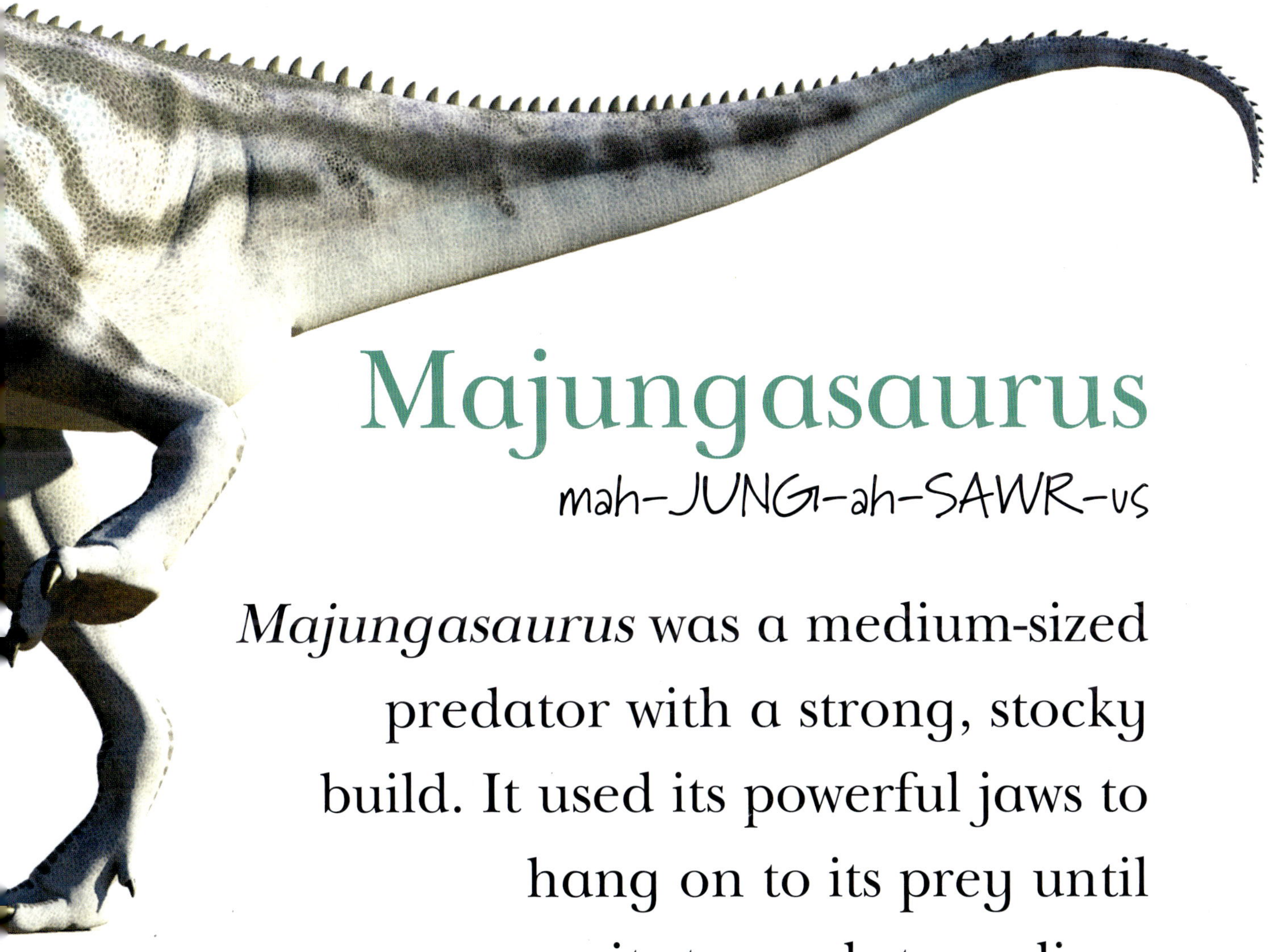

Majungasaurus
mah-JUNG-ah-SAWR-us

Majungasaurus was a medium-sized predator with a strong, stocky build. It used its powerful jaws to hang on to its prey until it stopped struggling.

Spinosaurus
SPY-nuh-SAWR-us

Spinosaurus is the largest of all the meat-eating dinosaurs. Its skull was long and narrow like a crocodile's, which was ideal for catching its favorite food…fish! It had a large sail on its back that acted like a car's radiator to keep it cool.

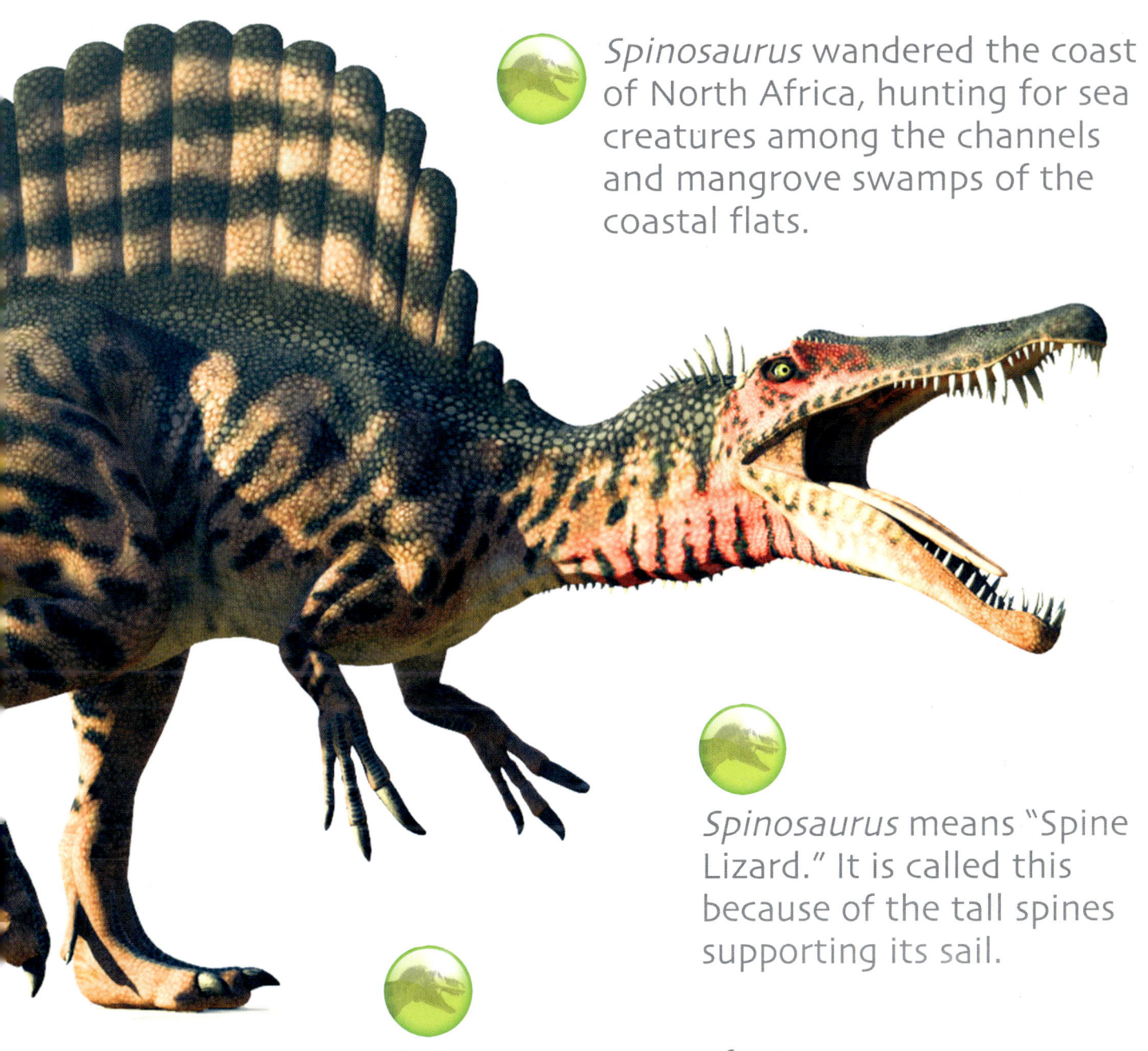

- *Spinosaurus* wandered the coast of North Africa, hunting for sea creatures among the channels and mangrove swamps of the coastal flats.

- *Spinosaurus* means "Spine Lizard." It is called this because of the tall spines supporting its sail.

- *Spinosaurus* was 59 feet (18 m) in length and 8 tons (7.3 metric tons) in weight.

Suchomimus

SOOK-o-MIME-us

This dinosaur's snout was similar to a crocodile's. Its jaw, crammed with backward-pointing teeth, was ideal for catching slippery, wriggling fish!

Suchomimus was 36 feet (11 m) in length and 4 tons (3.6 metric tons) in weight.

Suchomimus means "Crocodile Mimic."

Suchomimus hunted fish and other water creatures among the swamps and rivers of Niger in Africa. Its only enemies were giant crocodiles that lurked in the water.

Tarbosaurus means "Alarming Lizard."

Scientists found teeth marks from a *Tarbosaurus* on the fossil remains of a *Saurolophus*. They figured out that the *Saurolophus* was already dead when it was bitten, so *Tarbosaurus* was also a **scavenger**.

Tarbosaurus lived in China and Mongolia and was 33 feet (10 m) in length and 4 tons (3.6 metric tons) in weight.

Tarbosaurus
TAR-bow-SAWR-us

Tarbosaurus was a slightly smaller relative of *Tyrannosaurus rex*. It ambushed its prey, running a short distance before delivering a killing bite.

Tyrannosaurus rex lived in North America and measured up to 40 feet (12.2 m) in length, up to 13 feet (4 m) tall at the hips, and was around 7.5 tons (6.8 metric tons) in weight.

Tyrannosaurus means "Tyrant Lizard."

 *Tyrannosaurus rex* was a ferocious predator and scavenger. Its powerful jaws were crammed with 12-inch (30 cm) teeth that were as sharp as steak knives.

Tyrannosaurus rex
tye-RAN-uh-SAWR-us REKS

This dinosaur is the most famous of all. It had a massive skull balanced by a long, heavy tail. It had powerful legs and small arms with two fingers.

Glossary

cowlick
Hair on the head growing in a different direction from the rest and usually turned up or twisted.

predator
An animal that hunts and kills other animals for food.

scavenger
An animal that feeds on dead matter.

titanosaurs
A group of long-necked dinosaurs that included some of the heaviest animals ever to walk Earth.

Timeline

Dinosaurs lived during the Mesozoic Era, which is divided into three main periods.

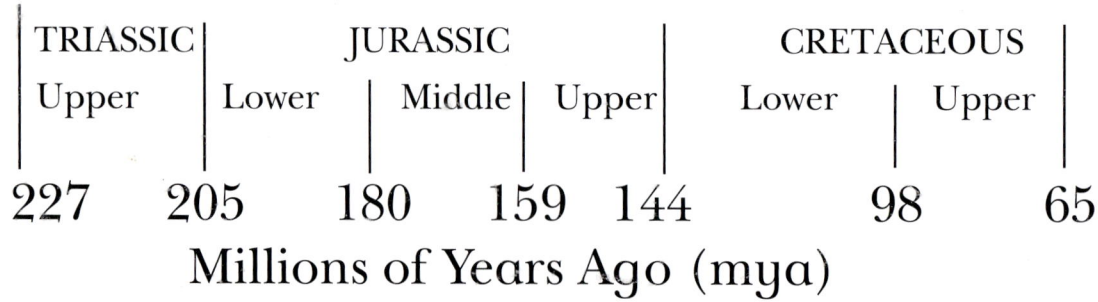